Stitch I

Jennie Rayment

Acknowledgements

This book is dedicated to my husband Nick and to all my friends and family especially my aunt Freda and uncle Richard who keep the bar open! I would not achieve all that I do without their tremendous support, help and large G and T's.

I thank most sincerely all the students who have suffered under my instruction and returned for more! Without the inspiration of teaching and the meeting of so many delightful people, my life would be very empty. Very grateful thanks to Daphne Leese for the penguin bunting, to my Emsworth Girls who made Tri-Totes and to young Harry Stone and Brenda Cottis for modelling.

Copyright © Jennie Rayment 2015
J. R. Publications
5 Queen Street, Emsworth,
Hampshire, PO10 7BJ. England, UK
Tel/Fax: +44 (0)1243 374860
e-mail: jenrayment@aol.com   web site: www.jennierayment.com

ISBN - 13: 978-0-9524675-0-2
ISBN - 10: 0-9524675-0-X

Printed by Holbrooks Printers Ltd
Norway Road, Hilsea
Portsmouth, Hampshire PO3 5HX
Tel: 02392 661485 Fax: 02392 671119 e-mail: mail@holbrooks.com

Fabrics for some projects: Craft Cotton Co.
http://craftcottonco.blogspot.co.uk/

Rotary cutters, rulers and mats:
EZ Quilting (Simplicity Creative Group)
PO Box 46, 1 Coronation Point,
Coronation Street, Stockport,
SK5 7PJ Tel: 0161 480 3355
www.Uk.eusales@simplicity.com

For excellent workshops, hilariously informative lectures and educational demonstrations with a world class teacher/lecturer contact Jennie:

Tel/Fax: +44 (0) 1243 374860
email: jenrayment@aol.com
web: jennierayment.com

J. R. Tri-Totes: Emsworth Girls

Contents

Fabric fun and pieceful play! Eighteen quick and easy projects from totes to soft boxes, Christmas crackers, festive decorations, bunting, pin cushions and sew much more. Ideal for all ages and abilities, this book will provide hours of fun and inspiration for further future ingenious creations.

Many of the designs can be hand sewn although use of a sewing machine is encouraged. For some ideas, a walking/even-feed foot attachment for the machine is useful but not essential. For accurate cutting of specific shapes and sizes, a rotary cutter, cutting mat and acrylic ruler are recommended. Most projects can be made from Fat Quarters or small scraps, so rummage in your stash and be creative.

Sit back, read the words, get out the fabric and you too can 'Stitch Bits' together!

Happy Twiddles

Jennie R

Contents

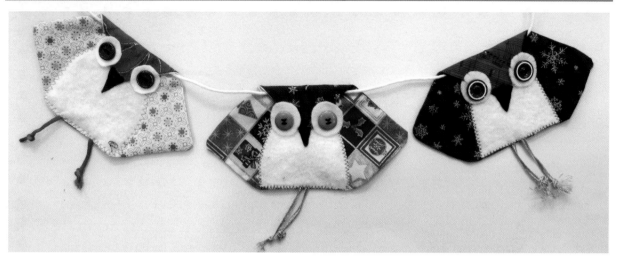

Owl Bunting

Size: 9 x 11 cm (**3½ x 4½"**) **S/A 0.65cm (¼")**

Forget traditional triangular bunting; make a row of cheery owls! Easy to sew, fun to create and oh sew different. Just get round twoo it!

Make one Owl:
Two 13cm (**5"**) squares - body
One 8cm (**3"**) square wadding/fleece/felt - chest
One 15cm (**6"**) thin ribbon or braid - feet
Two buttons, beads, felt scraps - eyes

1. Press one 13cm (**5"**) square in half diagonally. Open out. Press one corner to touch centre crease. Place pressed square R/S down on second 13cm (**5"**) square (R/S together).

2. Sew round outside edge of squares and across pressed crease. Trim excess fabric from corner.

3. Decide which fabric forms front of Owl. Slit this fabric carefully in centre. Turn Owl R/S out through the slit. Press carefully.

4. Fold 8cm (**3"**) square wadding or fleece/felt square in half. Cut corner to form arced shape.

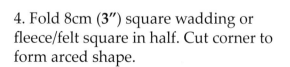

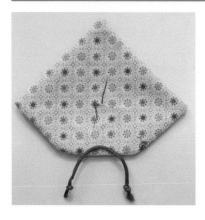

5. Tie a knot in both ends of 15cm (**6"**) thin ribbon or braid, fold in half and place on bottom of Owl front.

6. Lay the wadding shape over the feet. Pin in place.

7. Zigzag round edge of wadding shape. Match thread colour to wadding or try a contrasting coloured one for added interest.

8. Fold top of Owl over.

9. Cut small triangle of felt for beak. Sew beak in place through all layers.

10. Attach eyes: Cut two 2.5cm (**1"**) felt circles or thereabouts. (Draw round the base of a thread reel.)

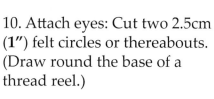

Lay felt circles on Owl's face. Sew a button or beads on top. Sew through all layers.

11. Thread cord through top of Owl and hang up. To stop Owls sliding about, attach top of Owl to cord with a few small stitches.

Now make another and another! You can change the colours, adjust the legs, alter the eyes and have a row of all different owls that are truly delightful. Your ingenious bunting will be viewed with a twit twoo and a wow!

5

Chicken Bunting

This is really silly! Festive fun for Easter and it's cheep!

Follow instructions for Owl Bunting (previous pages) but alter shape of the feet. Two small strips of orange felt were used here. The strips were cut roughly into a semblance of chick feet. (It has been said that they resemble the 'fish and chip' forks beloved by take-away eateries. Can you do better?)

And now for something even sillier!

Penguin Bunting

Size: 11 x 14cm (**4½ x 5½"**)
S/A 0.65cm (¼")

Make one Penguin:
One 11 x 46cm (**4½ x 18"**) - body
One 5 x 13cm (**2 x 5"**) wadding/felt or fleece - chest
One 5cm (**2"**) square felt - feet
Two buttons, beads, felt scraps - eyes

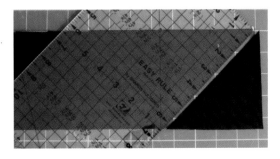

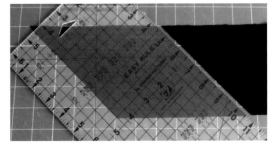

1. Place rotary cutting ruler on 11 x 46cm (**4½ x 18"**) strip aligning printed 45° line with top edge of fabric. Cut along edge of ruler. Turn fabric over. Use ruler to measure 11cm (**4½"**) from this cut edge. Cut along edge of ruler. This forms one diamond.

2. Working from this cut edge, cut second diamond.

3. Take one diamond, fold pointed end over to touch centre of diamond. Finger press fold. Draw chalk/pencil line along fold.

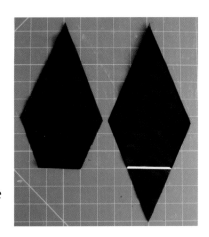

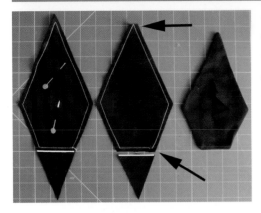

4. Lay both diamonds R/S together. Sew 0.65cm (¼") seam round outside edge and chalk line. Trim all excess fabric carefully to stitching line. Make a slit in centre of penguin and turn R/S out. Poke corners out gently. Press.

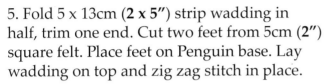

5. Fold 5 x 13cm (**2 x 5"**) strip wadding in half, trim one end. Cut two feet from 5cm (**2"**) square felt. Place feet on Penguin base. Lay wadding on top and zig zag stitch in place.

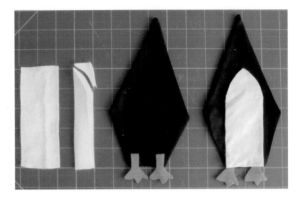

6. Fold top of Penguin over. Cut small beak from leftover felt scraps. Cut two small circles for eyes. Attach eyes in place with beads or buttons. Sew through all layers.

7. Thread cord through top of Penguin. Secure penguin head to cord with small stitches to stop penguin sliding along cord.

To complete this section ...

A local copper is amazed to see a man drive past with a car full of penguins. He stops the car and says "Excuse me sir, you shouldn't be driving round with those penguins - take them to the zoo." The man does that.

The next day, the policeman is astounded to see the man drive past again - still with his car full of penguins. He stops the car. "Here, I thought I told you to take those penguins to the zoo!" "I did," replies the man. "We had so much fun that we're going to the beach today!"

Rooster Pincushion

Size: 10 x 9 cm (4 x 3½")
S/A 0.65cm (¼")

Utilise odd strips of fabric and felt scraps to create a rotund rooster!

Make one Rooster:
Two 4.5cm (1¾") squares - head
Four 2.5 x 45cm (1 x 18") - middle body
One 3 x 50cm (1¼ x 20") - outer body
One 6.5cm (2½") square - tail
Two buttons/beads/felt scraps - eyes
Felt scraps - coxcomb/beak/wattle
Wadding pieces + dried pulses - stuffing

1. From one 2.5cm (1") body strip cut 4.5cm (1¾") strip. Attach this strip to one side of 4.5cm (1¾") square. Open out. Press seam to outside edge.

2. Turn block anticlockwise. Measure side of block. Cut another strip this length. Attach to side of block. Open out. Press seam to outside edge.

3. Measure side of block. From second body strip, cut strip this length. Attach to side of block. Open out. Press seam to outside edge.

4. Repeat Stage 2 with same body strip.

5. Repeat Stages 3 - 4 twice more using remaining two Rooster body strips. Press carefully between each set of strips.

6. Take 3 x 50cm (1¼ x 20") outer body strip. Repeat Stages 3 - 4.

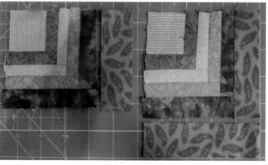

7. Take second 4.5cm (1¾″) head square. Follow Stages 1 - 6 to make other side of Rooster.

8. If necessary square up both sections to same measurement.

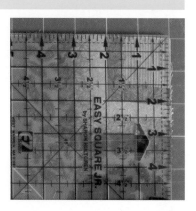

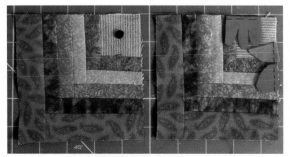

9. From scraps of felt, cut beak, coxcomb, wattle and two eyes. Attach one felt eye to middle of each side of head.

Sew beak, coxcomb and wattle (all facing inwards) to one side of Rooster's head.

10. Lay both halves of Rooster R/S together. Pin layers carefully. Match seams if possible but don't panic if they won't, does it really matter?

11. Start stitching along Rooster back. Curve stitching very gently around head corner. Curve stitching slightly more on next corner. Stop stitching at end of third side (see photograph). Leave last side completely open.

12. Turn Rooster R/S out. Flatten Rooster to form a 'humbug' shape - sort of triangle. Stuff Rooster with torn scraps of wadding and any combination of pulses/rice or beans. Line body with wadding scraps first before adding any heavier stuffing.

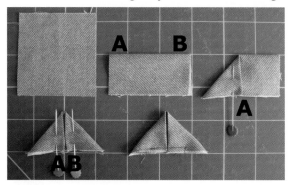

13. Fold 6.5cm (2½″) tail square in half R/S out. Bring top of fold at **A** to the centre, repeat on the other side making a triangle. Sew across base of triangle. Insert tail into back of Rooster. Close the hole with small hand stitches.

14. Stick a few pins in!

P.S. If using a dried pulse or pea stuffing - don't wash the Rooster. The dried veg might start sprouting and then you will have a very strange pin cushion!

Wrist Pincushion

Make one Pincushion:
Two 10cm (**4"**) squares felt
One 20cm (**8"**) 12mm (**½"**) elastic
One 4.5cm (**1¾"**) circle thick card
Wadding pieces - stuffing

1. Draw 8cm (**3"**) circle on one felt square. (Draw round a mug if no compass to hand.)

2. Cut 0.65cm (**¼"**) outside drawn line. From second square, cut same sized circle.

3. Sew decorative patterns on one felt circle. (If using machine, edge of presser foot follows drawn line.)

4. Measure circumference of wrist. Cut elastic this length. Sew elastic to centre of second felt circle.

5. Put both circles together R/S out. Sew round on drawn line - leave 4.5cm (**1¾"**) gap.

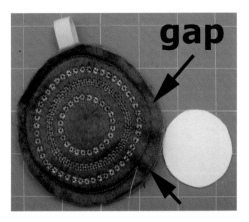

gap

6. Insert card into pincushion. Stuff pincushion firmly. Keep stuffing between card and top of pincushion - the card prevents sharp pin points from puncturing your wrist.

7. Close the gap: Attach zipper foot to machine, set needle position to left of presser foot. Sew across gap following drawn line.

Alternatively hand sew along drawn line.

8. Trim excess felt on outside of pincushion close to stitching line with pinking shears.

And finally ... stick pins in!

Happy Caterpillar

Approx size: 10 x 36cm (**4 x 14″**)

This creepy crawlie can be any size and length. Make a baby one for a young child. Add many more 'segments' for an ingenious draught excluder. Use all those remnants lurking in your stash, re-cycle old clothes and materials - each segment could remind you of some special event or time.

Make one Caterpillar:
Twenty-two 20cm (**8″**)* diameter circles - body
One 60cm (**24″**) square wadding - stuffing
Two 8cm (**3″**) squares felt - face
One 10cm (**4″**) square felt - tail
One 6 x 13cm (**2½ x 5″**) felt - fringe/hat
One 45cm (**18″**) 12mm (**½″**) elastic
Felt scraps - face
* *This measurement is not crucial. Why not use a plate or any other round household object of similar diameter as a template?*

8″

stitch

1. Sew close to raw edge of one circle. Pull the thread through and gather fabric. Do not finish off stitching, leave thread loose. Flatten fabric to form a smaller circle.

2. Cut rough circle of wadding a little smaller than the flattened fabric. Slacken the stitching, tuck wadding inside fabric circle. Pull thread tight and fasten off.

3. Insert small sharp scissors through centre. Snip through all layers making small 1cm (**½″**) slit.

4. Repeat Stages 1 - 3 with all remaining fabric circles.

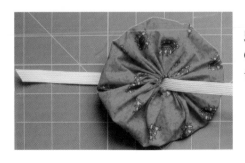

5. Thread elastic through slit. Continue threading elastic through every other circle.

6. Cut 10cm (**4"**) felt square into rough circle. Sew round edge. Stuff with oddments of wadding until it forms a ball. Attach this ball to one end of the elastic.

7. Cut both 8cm (**3"**) squares into circles (draw round mug or cup).

8. Cut eyes and mouth from felt scraps. Stitch features on one of the circles.

9. Sew both circles together R/S out. Leave a small gap in stitching. Stuff wadding scraps through gap. Close gap with small stitches.

10. Pin 6 x 13cm (**2½ x 5"**) strip to top of head.

Arrange as small cap, and sew in place or sew felt strip to head and clip to form fuzzy fringe.

11. Sew head to other end of elastic.

Now make a friend - who knows what they may get up to?

And to make you groan...

How do caterpillars order their latest outfit?

From a caterlogue!

Nifty Handbag

Size: 22 x 24cm (**9 x 9½"**)
S/A 0.65cm (¼")

From two rectangles and some wadding, create a simple lined hand or shoulder bag with a flat bottom! Follow the instructions, look at the photographs to reveal this natty method.

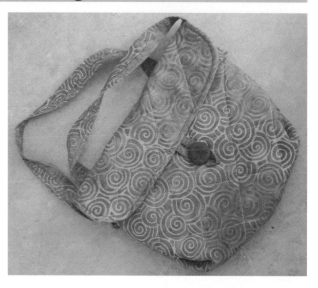

Make one Handbag:
One 25 x 53cm (**10 x 21"**) bag
One 25 x 53cm (**10 x 21"**) lining
One 3 x 11cm (**1¼ x 4½"**) tab
One 6 x 112cm (**2½ x 42"**) handle
One 30 x 60cm (**12 x 23"**) wadding: One button

1. Place 25 x 53cm (**10 x 21"**) strip (bag exterior) on wadding R/S up. Pin layers.

2. Quilt layers together: This can be done with free motion stipple (wiggle) over the surface or by cross hatching using a quilting guide. Alternatively quilt layers with any arrangement of stitched lines using regular presser foot.

Cross Hatching:
Align 45° line (printed on acrylic ruler) with straight edge of fabric. Draw line along edge of ruler. Chalk, pencil, wash-out marking pens are good choices. Increase straight stitch length to 3 - 3.5mm. Sew along drawn line.

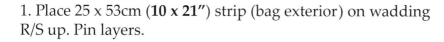

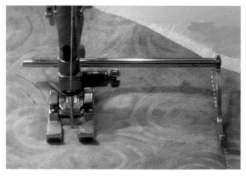

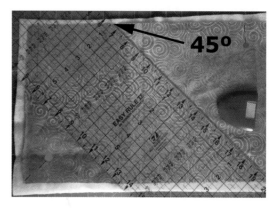

Attach quilting guide to presser foot. Place end of guide on first row of stitches as shown. Sew the second line. Both stitched lines are parallel and are width of guide apart.

Continue to work in the same manner. The guide follows previous line of stitching at all times. Watch the guide carefully.

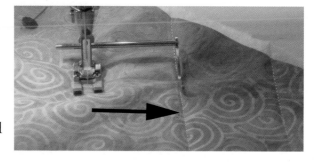

Turn fabric round. Align end of guide with first row of stitches and work to other edge of panel as described above. A diagonal grid of stitched lines is created.

Nifty Handbag

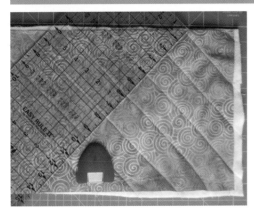

Place ruler on fabric. Align parallel lines on ruler with stitched rows. Drawn a second line. Work from this drawn line as described on previous page.

A diagonally stitched square pattern is formed. This is known as cross hatching. (*If no quilting guide, draw evenly spaced parallel lines across fabric, sew on lines.*)

3. Trim excess wadding from edge of panel.

4. Sew 0.65cm (¼″) hem on one 25cm (**10″**) edge.

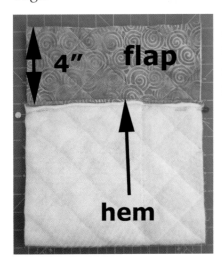

5. Fold quilted section R/S together. Position hemmed edge 10cm (**4″**) away from one end as shown. This folded section forms the 'body' of the bag. (The exposed section is the bag flap.)

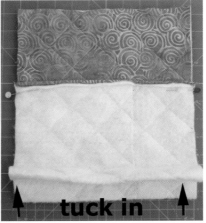

6. Tuck folded edge 3cm (1¼″) inwards. Pin tuck in place. This tuck creates the flat base of the bag.

7. Sew both sides. Stitch slowly over tucked sections.

8. Repeat Stages 4 - 7 with lining **BUT** increase depth of tucked section to **3.5cm (1½″)**.

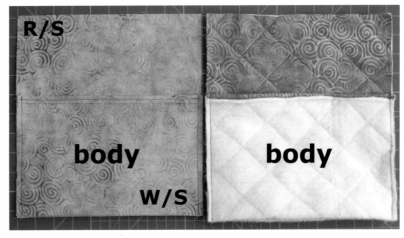

Making a bag lining shorter in length than bag exterior ensures that the lining fits neatly inside.

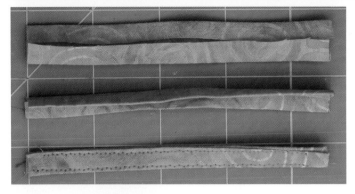

9. Make tab:
Fold both long sides of 3 x 11cm (1¼ x 14½″) strip to centre. Fold this strip in half again. Sew close to both sides.

10. Sew tab in centre of flap section.

11. Trim corners of flap section in gentle arc. (Draw round reel of sticky tape or cup or round tin.)

flap

sew

Make Up Handbag

Have faith... Follow the instructions!

1. Lay lining section on bag. **Both 'body' sections face each other on inside.** Pin layers.

2. Start stitching just below top of body section. Sew round flap and finish just past top of body section on the other side of the flap.

3. Turn bag flap R/S out.

4. Turn bag outside section R/S out. With gentle persuasion, the bottom corners of the handbag will open to form a triangular shape.

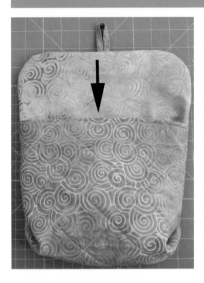

5. Tuck lining inside the handbag.

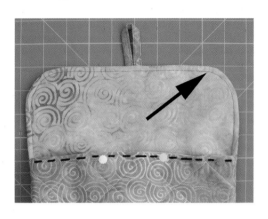

6. Press flap of bag and top stitch 0.65cm (¼″) from outside edge.

7. Close the gap between the bag and the lining with hand or machine stitches.

Make Handle

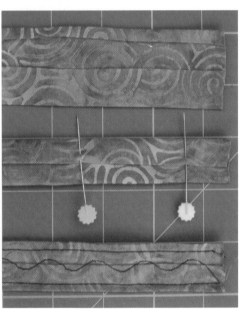

1. Take 6 x 53cm (**2½ x 21″**) handle strip and press one long edge 0.65cm (¼″) to W/S.

2. Press opposite edge of same strip 2cm (¾″) to W/S.

3. Fold 0.65cm (¼″) edge over to overlap the opposite side. Press. Pin layers.

4. Select a wide decorative stitch. Sew centre of strip. Straight stitch along both sides.

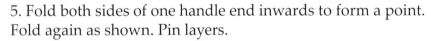

5. Fold both sides of one handle end inwards to form a point. Fold again as shown. Pin layers.

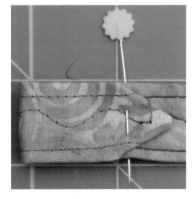

Repeat with other end.

6. Attach handle ends to opposite sides of bag.

7. Attach the button.

Pop purse inside and you are good to go!

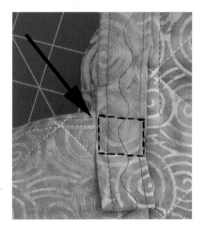

J. R. Tri-Tote

Maximum size: 28 x 61cm (**11 x 24"**)
S/A 0.65cm (¼")

Going shopping, lots to buy? You
need a Tri-Tote. Why? This bag
expands and holds more than you
think. Tri-Tote? It's made from
triangles! J. R? My idea!

Make one Tri-Tote:
Three 30.5 x 56cm (**12 x 22"**) - bag
Two 30.5 x 74cm (**12 x 29"**) - lining
Two 9 x 56cm (**3½ x 22"**) - handles
Two 6 x 20cm (**2½ x 8"**) - tabs
Two 33 x 74cm (**13 x 29"**) wadding
Two 3.5 x 56cm (**1½ x 22"**) wadding
1.5 x 6cm ($^5/_8$ x **2½"**) hook and loop fastener (Velcro)

1. For Tri-Tote bag:
Cut two 60° triangles from each of the three 30.5 x 56cm (**12 x 22"**) strips.

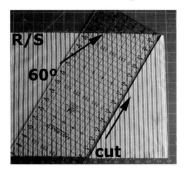
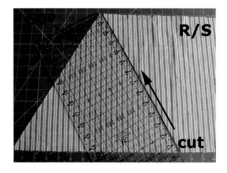
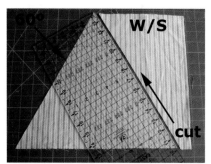

Place 60° line on straight edge of fabric (R/S up). Cut along edge of ruler. Turn fabric
round, replace ruler aligning 60° line with this cut edge, cut again. This makes the first
triangle. Flip fabric over to W/S, replace ruler. Align 60° line as shown, cut again. Two
60° triangles are now cut out. (Left handed students - hold book to a mirror and follow
pictures.)

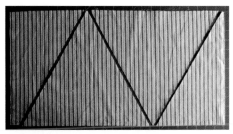

Repeat with remaining two 30.5 x 56cm (**12 x 22"**) bag
strips making six triangles in total.

*If struggling - cut one fabric triangle. Use this as a template
for the remaining shapes.*

*OR: Make a useful template from 30.5 x 35.5cm (12 x 14") sheet
of card/heavy paper. Mark midpoint on 35.5cm (14") side. Draw
a line from this mark to both opposite corners. Cut out shape.
(This triangle is almost 100% accurate and will work admirably.)*

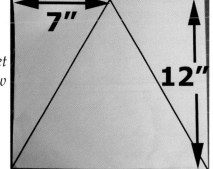

OR: Purchase Sew Easy 12" 60° triangle template!

2. Lay out three triangles as shown.

Check that the straight grain of each triangle (non stretchy side) is placed where indicated by arrows.

3. Sew three triangles together. Press seams open and flat.

4. Repeat with remaining three triangles. (Both sections must be the same.)

These two sections are tote sides.

5. Lay one tote side on a wadding section, cut round leaving a small margin of wadding. Pin layers together.

6. Quilt tote side to wadding. For simplicity, sew either side of seams.

7. Using a long stitch length, sew round outside edges, keep stitching close to raw edge.

8. Repeat Stages 5 - 7 with other half of tote.

Lining

1. Cut three triangles from both 30.5 x 74cm (**12 x 29"**) strips.

2. Check position of straight grain before sewing the three triangles together. Press seams open and flat.

Handles

1. Press 0.65mm (¼ ") fold to W/S along one long side of one handle strip. Fold and press the opposite side over to W/S by about 2.5cm (**1"**).

Press fabric again so first fold overlaps the other side. This folded edge should lie in centre of band.

Open band and lay wadding strip inside. Fold fabric over. Pin layers.

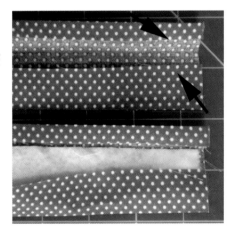

2. Select a simple machine decorative stitch, increase stitch width to maximum. (A wide zigzag can be substituted if no decorative stitches available on your machine.)

Sew down the centre of the strip. More stitches can be added to either side if desired.

Tabs

1. Make two tabs from 6 x 20cm (**2½ x 8″**) strips. Follow handle method but omit the wadding.

2. Fold each tab in half. Attach one section of hook and loop fastener to each tab.

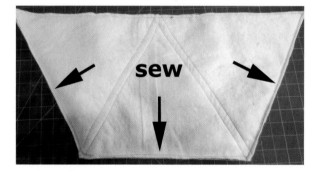

Sew Tote Together

1. Sew one handle to each side of tote. R/S of handle to R/S of tote. Keep stitching inside 6.5mm (¼″) S/A.

2. Sew both halves of tote together. Sew sides and base as indicated by arrows.

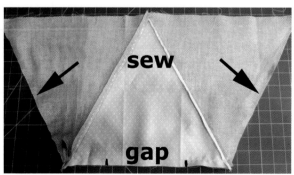

3. Attach one tab to each top corner of tote. Make sure tote seam is open and flat.

Remember to place one tab with hook and loop side up and the other with hook and loop underneath.

4. Sew lining sections together. Leave a gap in the base of the lining sections.

Take a larger 1.5cm (½″) seam allowance when sewing the base - this action ensures that the lining lies neatly inside tote.

5. Insert tote outside section into the lining, both R/S together. Match raw edges along the top. Pin carefully.

6. Sew round top of tote.

7. Turn tote R/S out through the gap in the lining.

8. Tuck lining inside tote.

9. Press top edge of tote carefully. Stitch round top of tote.

10. Close the gap in the lining with small hand or machine stitches.

11. Fasten hook and loop tabs. This draws the sides of the tote inwards.

12. Sling tote over shoulder and go shopping and when you indulge in mega amounts of retail therapy, undo the tabs and enlarge the bag!

'Stitch and Flip' Crazy Patchwork Tri-Tote using fabric scraps

1. Construct a card template (page 17).

2. Cut six triangles approximately 2.5cm (**1"**) larger than card template from light weight interfacing or other thin material such as calico/muslin.

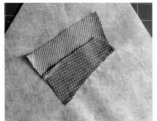

3. Lay fabric scrap R/S up on centre of one interfacing triangle. Place second piece of fabric R/S down, stitch along edge and flip back (as shown). Place third piece R/S down on top, stitch etc. and flip back. Continue working in this manner until interfacing or thin fabric is covered. For total success, each additional strip must be long enough to cover both ends of underlying section.

4. On completion, place card template on top and trim any excess fabric to edge of template.

5. Repeat Stages 3 - 4 five times to make six triangles in total.

6. Follow Stage 3 page 18 and complete Tri-Tote.

For extra security add a tab:

Make 6 - 8cm (**2½ - 3"**) tab (see Stage 5 page 43). Stitch tab to one side of Tri-Tote when attaching the handles (Stage 1 page 19). Sew small section of hook fastener to tab.

On completion of Tri-Tote, stitch loop fastener in correct place on outside side of Tri-Tote.

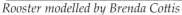

Rooster modelled by Brenda Cottis

Chicken Fun

Make a bigger Rooster by cutting the head square larger and increasing the width of the strips. This could be a silly gift for a friend!

Alternatively, make an enormous Rooster from two Log Cabin* Squares sewn together as shown above.
For Log Cabin technique watch Eazy Peazy Patchwork DVD.

Now for something silly....

What do you call a chicken crossing the road? Poultry in motion.

A lady was picking through the frozen chickens in a supermarket but she couldn't find one big enough for her family.

She asked a passing assistant, "Do these chickens get any bigger?"
The assistant replied, "I'm afraid not, Madam, they're dead."

J. R. Tri-Totes: Emsworth Girls

Four from One!

The title says it all. Fold a square into three different bag designs or into a soft padded box. It's origami in material! Fabric fun for fiddly fingers.

Triple Pocket Bag *(top left in picture)*

Size: 21cm (**8¼″**) square
S/A 0.65cm (¼″)

Make one Triple Pocket Bag:
One 46.5cm (**18½″**) square - bag
One 46.5cm (**18½″**) square - lining
One 49cm (**19½″**) square wadding
Two 3 x 10cm (**1¼ x 4″**) - tabs
One 6 x 112cm (**2½ x 44″**) - handle
Two buttons/beads

1. From 3 x 10cm (**1¼ x 4″**) strips make two tabs (Stage 9 page 15).

2. Place lining on wadding. Pin layers. Attach one tab to opposite corners.

3. Lay other square (bag section) on top, R/S together. Align both fabrics on raw edges.

4. Sew round outside edge of both fabrics. LEAVE a GAP on one side - gap should be away from tabs.

5. Turn bag R/S out through gap. Press well. Close gap with small hand or machine stitches.

6. Top stitch round square 0.65cm (¼″) from edge.

23

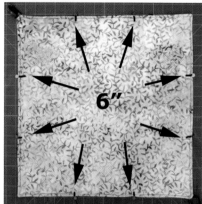

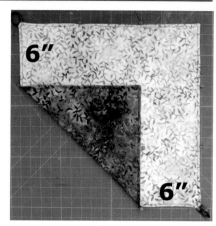

7. Use pins to mark all four sides at 15cm (**6"**) intervals.

8. Fold one corner over. Make sure the fold is on 15cm (**6"**) marker pins.

9. Repeat on opposite corner. Align all marker pins. Both opposite corners overlap. A lozenge shape is formed.

10. Select a straight or decorative machine stitch and sew the top two layers together where they overlap (right-hand picture).

BE CAREFUL, only sew top two layers.

To make sewing process easier:
Remove any sewing machine extension table and use the free arm facility if available. The two layers will still need some wriggling to get them in place under the presser foot due to the awkward angle of seam. If in doubt - sew both layers firmly by hand.

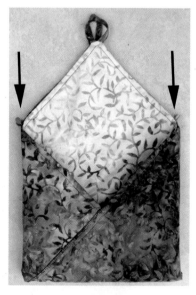

11. Fold lozenge in half aligning all edges. This makes the bag.

12. Sew down both sides of bag by hand. Use a firm blanket stitch or similar pattern.

Alternatively, use a zigzag stitch on machine:

Set **widest** stitch width, stitch length at regular (2.5mm). Place side of bag just underneath left hand edge of presser foot.

Start sewing. Left needle position goes in fabric, right needle position is off material into thin air! The thread will automatically close up to fabric edge. Experiment on a scrap if not sure.

13. Take 6 x 112cm (**2½ x 44"**) strip and make handle (page 16). Attach one handle end to each side of bag.

14. Fold one flap down. Mark position of button. Sew button in place. Repeat on other side of bag.

Now you can see why it is a triple pocket bag... There is another pocket in the centre. Magic!

This intriguing design can be made with any size of square:

Decide on size of square. Divide sides of square into thirds. Follow this method.

You can make a giant Triple Pocket Bag or just a little one.

Play!

Speedy Bagette!

Size: 20 x 36cm (**8 x 14"**)
S/A 0.65cm (¼")

Make one Speedy Bagette:
One 46.5cm (**18½"**) square - bag
One 46.5cm (**18½"**) square - lining
One 49cm (**19½"**) square wadding
One 3 x 10cm (**1¼ x 4"**) - tab
One 6 x 112cm (**2½ x 44"**) - handle
One button/bead

1. Follow Stages 1 - 6 page 23 BUT insert one tab only.

2. Fold square in half diagonally making a triangle, make sure tab is at one end of triangle as shown.

3. Oversew side of triangle (see picture) using slightly loose stitching. (This loose stitching ensures both sides of the triangle lie flush when the triangle is flattened.)

4. Flatten triangle into a kite shaped bag.

5. Fold sharp pointed end of kite shape over by 5cm (**2"**).

6. Refold this edge to touch top of bag. Sew through all top layers (see below).

Warning: There are many layers to sew through; insert heavyweight sewing machine needle (14/90 or 16/100). Increase stitch length to 3.5mm. Or sew by hand with stronger thread (30 - 40wt), large eyed heavy-duty needle. (A thimble may be useful.)

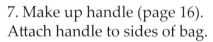

7. Make up handle (page 16). Attach handle to sides of bag.

8. Fold flap over, mark position of button. Sew button in place.

For speedy button sewing, thread large eyed needle with several strands of thread.

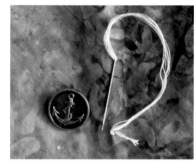

Posh Clutch

Size: 18 x 31cm (**7 x 12½"**)
S/A 0.65cm (¼")

Make one Posh Clutch:
One 46.5cm (**18½"**) square - bag
One 46.5cm (**18½"**) square - lining
One 49cm (**19½"**) square wadding
One 3 x 10cm (**1¼ x 4"**) - tab
One button/bead

1. Follow Stages 1 - 6 page 23 BUT insert one tab only.

To make this bag a little firmer and more decorative, consider quilting the square before making up the bag. Try free motion stippling or cross hatching. If cross hatching the walking foot must be used to prevent the layers creeping. (Cross hatching page 13.) This Posh Clutch was constructed with a free motion quilted square.

2. Mark midpoints of all four sides.

3. Fold square in half diagonally matching midpoints.

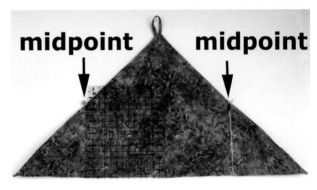

4. Draw a line on either side from the midpoints to base of triangle.

This line can be drawn with any medium - the line will be covered up afterwards.

5. Sew along both drawn lines. A flap is formed.

6. Open one flap and fold back.

The flap folds back over stitching on both sides.

Repeat on other side of bag.

7. At tab end of Posh Clutch, there are two flaps. Fold the flap without a tab down first. Secure this flap to the front of Posh Clutch with the button.

8. Now fold tab flap over and fasten bag.

If you prefer bags with handles, cut one 6 x 112cm (**2½ x 44"**) strip. Make up handle (page 16). Attach handle to sides of Posh Clutch.

Why not make a smaller one in Christmas fabrics or make one in velvet/silk/satin to match your posh frock?

*Posh Clutch with handle and Speedy Bagette made from 38cm (**15"**) squares: Jennie Rayment*

Padded Box

Size: 11 x 21cm (**4½" x 8"**)
S/A 0.65cm (¼")

A useful bit of kit! It is reversible - the pockets can be internal or external, it can be closed with a draw string. The technique would work with any size of square. More magic!

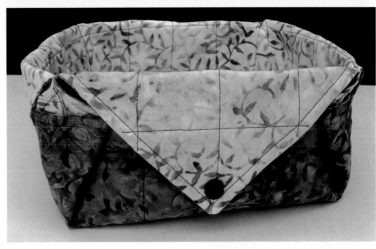

Make one Padded Box:
Two 46.5cm (**18½"**) squares
One 49cm (**19½"**) square wadding
Four buttons/beads

1. Follow Stages 1 - 6 page 23 but **don't add tabs.**

The padded box is best quilted. Either free motion stipple, cross hatch (page 13) or create a similar line design. Use a walking foot or free motion foot to prevent the layers creeping.

2. Mark sides of square at 15cm (**6"**) intervals.

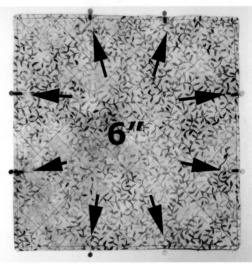

3. Fold square in half forming a rectangle. Match marker pins.

4. Draw a 45° line from 6" marker pin to folded edge of rectangle. Place 45° line (printed on ruler) along edge of fabric.

The line will not show so any drawing medium can be used. Sew along drawn line. Repeat on the other side. Two triangular tucks are formed on opposite sides of the folded square.

5. Refold the square on the other two sides and repeat Stage 4.

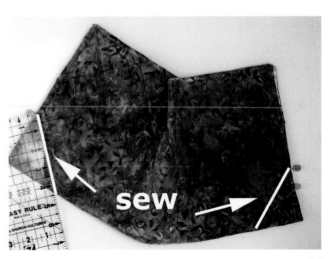

Four triangular pockets are created.

6. Flatten the pockets. Secure top corners of each pocket with small hand stitches through all layers.

7. Fold the flap back. Secure in place with a button.

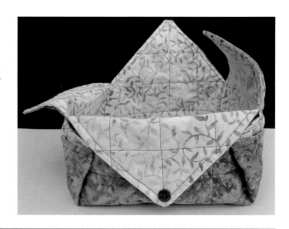

Behold - a padded box!

Consider turning the box the other way out at Stage 6 and having the pockets on the inside, then securing the flaps.

Why not forget folding the flaps completely? Fold them over about 4cm (1½"); secure tips of flaps with a button. Thread a cord though. Now you can draw the top of the box together.

You can make this box any size by simply dividing the sides of the initial quilted square in thirds and following these instructions.

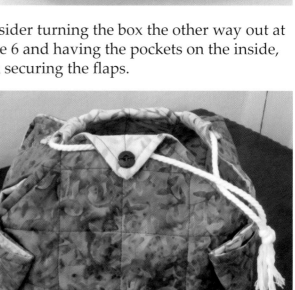

Hexagonal Happening

Size: 10cm (**4"**) diameter

A stiffened tucked and twiddled hexagon double sided novelty. Ideal as a Christmas decoration. Another ingenious design from Jennie's inventive imagination!

Make one Hexagonal Happening:
Two 23 x 26cm (**9 x 10"**) fabric
One 11 x 13cm (**4½ x 5"**) craft Vilene (Pellon) or stiff interfacing
One 15cm (**6"**) thin ribbon
One 11 x 13cm (**4½ x 5"**) thin card
Two buttons/beads/sequins
A4 sheet paper, ruler, paper glue

1. Make template for stiff hexagon: Trace or photocopy template. Cut out tracing/photocopy and stick on thin card. Cut round shape.

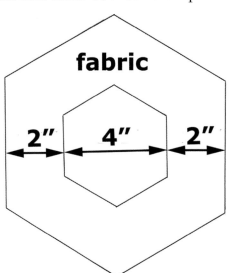

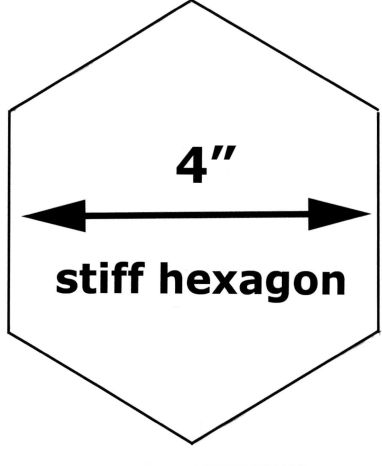

2. Make fabric template:
Place card template from Stage 1 on centre of A4 paper. Draw round.
Rule a line 5cm (**2"**) away from all sides of this drawn hexagon. Cut out the large hexagon shape on the outside line. *The large hexagon is used as the __fabric template__.*

3. Using card template for stiff hexagon: Cut one hexagon from 11 x 13cm (**4½ x 5"**) craft Vilene (Pellon) or stiff interfacing.

4. Using fabric template: Cut one hexagon from both 23 x 26cm (**9 x 10"**) fabrics.

31

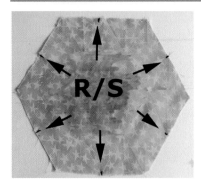

5. On **R/S** of both fabric hexagons, mark mid point of each side. Mark points clearly.

6. On **W/S** of one fabric hexagon, draw lines from corner to corner.

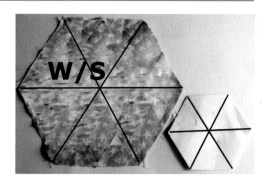

7. On one side of the stiff hexagon, draw lines across shape from corner to corner.

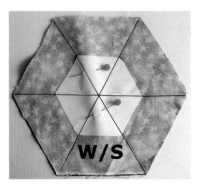

8. **Lay both fabric hexagons R/S together**. Place stiff hexagon on top aligning all drawn lines. Pin layers.

9. Working only on stiff hexagon, sew every line. Lock stitching at start and end of each line of stitch.

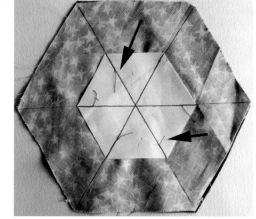

If no lock/fix setting on machine, begin stitching approx 1.5cm (½″) from start of line, reverse to start then sew along line, repeat this manoeuvre at the other end. Hand sewers should make firm back stitches at both ends of each line.

10. Fold opposite sides of top fabric hexagon to touch in centre. The marked midpoints will align. Using small machine stitches or hand stitches sew across the marked midpoints. Sew through all layers.

11. Take next side of hexagon. Fold fabric over and bring midpoint to touch centre. Stitch in place with small stitches.

12. Repeat with next side.

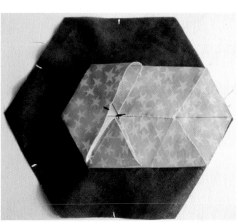

13. Continue until all six midpoints touch at hexagon centre and are sewn in place. Six triangular flaps are formed. Press well

14. Take one flap, open and flatten into kite shape.

15. Pull tip of flap firmly back towards outside edge of hexagon. It forms a diamond shape. Gently press shape.

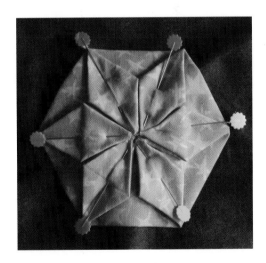

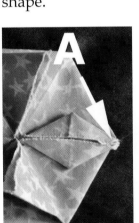

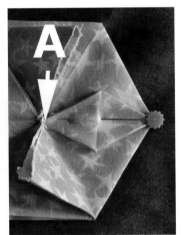

16. Fold diamond in half. Bring tip of diamond (**A**) to touch centre of hexagon.

17. Repeat with all other flaps.

18. Carefully sew tips of flaps in place through all layers.

Now for the other fabric hexagon ...

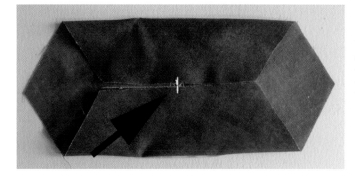

19. Working on second fabric hexagon, bring sides to middle. Sew in place through all layers.

20. Continue following Stages 11 - 18.

21. Insert the thin ribbon between both hexagons. Sew in place.

22. Cover centre stitching with a button/beads/sequins.

Why not make a matching button?

Take old button or small coin. Cut one fabric circle a little larger than coin or button. Gather edge of fabric circle, insert the coin/button. Draw up thread. Finish off. Sew in place.

Alternatively create a fluffy thread flower.

Thread machine with a different colour on top spool and in bobbin. If selecting a metallic thread, place this in bobbin (thread should snap less frequently... With luck!).

Insert medium weight calico or similar cloth into embroidery hoop. Pull fabric drum tight.

Cut 2.5 - 4cm (**1 - 1½"**) hole.

Attach free motion, darning/hopper foot to sewing machine.

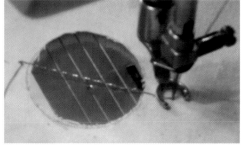

Take courage in both hands! Sew across the hole.

To get a good fluffy flower, run the machine slowly and move the hoop quickly - top and bottom threads should not be too tightly wrapped around each other. This might take a little practise.

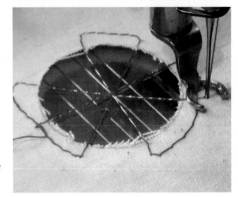

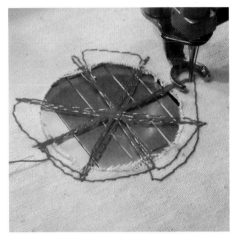

Sew across hole four times, North to South, West to East and in between these points.

Re-sew over these four lines several times.

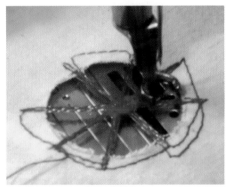

In centre, stitch round and round to make a hub.

Sew from hub to edge until hole is covered. More lines of stitch will make a fluffier flower.

Cut out flower.

Make another in same hole. It is a re-usable hole!

Consider sewing several Hexagonal Happenings together to create a double sided panel.

Or make a Hexagonal Happening single sided (omit second hexagon). Apply this starry delight to a quilt/garment/box etc.

Double Duty Cracker

Size: 6 x 37cm (**2½ x 14½"**)
S/A 0.65cm (¼")

Enhance the festive table with handsome hand crafted crackers. Once admired, unwrap, reveal the gift, motto and silly hat (or not!), open out to make a place mat. Fun, **festive** and fabulous! Gather odd strips and square-ish scraps, then 'Stitch 'n Flip'!

Make one Cracker:
Selection of strips: 4cm - 7cm x 18 - 44cm (**1½ - 2½" x 7 - 18"**)
One 10 - 15cm (**4 - 6"**) square
One 29 x 38cm (**11½ x 15"**) wadding
One 29 x 38cm (**11½ x 15"**) backing
One 29 x 38cm (**11½ x 15"**) light-weight sew in interfacing
One 29 x 38cm (**11½ x 15"**) wadding
4.5 x 132cm (**1¾ x 52"**) binding (join strips if necessary)
100cm (**36"**) ribbon + 13 x 5cm (**5 x 2"**) card tube

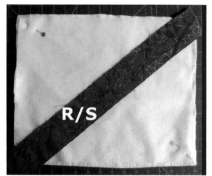

1. Place interfacing on wadding. Pin both layers. Lay first strip R/S up diagonally across the layers. Trim strip to size if necessary.

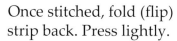

2. Take second strip, place R/S down (W/S up). Trim to size. Pin layers well. Sew strip in place.

Once stitched, fold (flip) strip back. Press lightly.

3. Continue working in same fashion, pinning and pressing each additional sewn strip. Stop short distance from corner. Cut triangular section from 10 - 15cm (**4 - 6"**) square to cover the corner. Sew triangle in place.

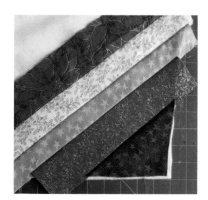

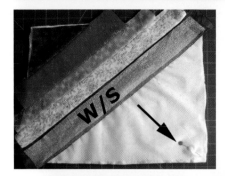

4. Turn work round. Cover remainder of interfacing and wadding as described in Stages 2 - 3.

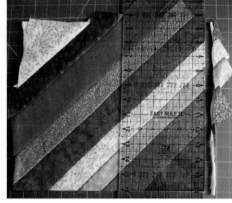

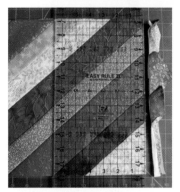

5. Trim panel to 28 x 37cm (**11 x 14½″**): Place work on cutting mat, align panel with lines on mat. Trim one side, turn work, trim each subsequent side until correct size is reached.

6. Lay trimmed Cracker panel on backing fabric. Pin layers. Sew round outside edge using long stitch length. This secures all layers. Trim excess backing fabric to edge of Cracker panel.

Binding

There are several ways to attach binding. Here is one method.

1. Place binding on centre of one side. Align raw edges. Use 1 cm (³/₈″) S/A. (On many machines this is marked on the throat plate.) Commence stitching 6cm (**2½″**) from start of binding.

2. Sew to 5cm (**2″**) from corner. Fold binding exactly round corner of Cracker panel. A triangle is formed.

3. Fold triangle from side to side and finger-press crease firmly.

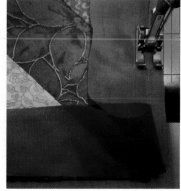

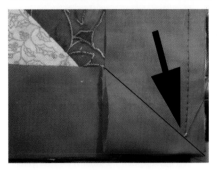

4. Sew to edge of triangle - do not sew one stitch further - STOP!

5. Remove work from under presser foot. Turn Cracker panel, fold triangle over to other side.

6. Start stitching on corner of Cracker panel and sew over triangle as shown.

7. Continue sewing round panel edge repeating above stages on every corner until you reach start of binding.

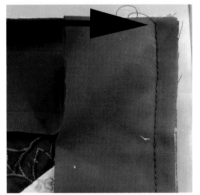

8. Join ends together:
At start of binding, fold 0.65cm (¼") to W/S. Lay end of binding on top, trim excess fabric until binding end overlaps binding start by approximately 1cm (½"). Sew over junction.

9. Press binding carefully over edge of Cracker to back. Amazingly a mitre forms on the front.

10. Fold binding over to backing fabric.

11. Fold raw edge 1 cm (³/₈") to W/S of binding. Fold corner of binding into mitre. Slip or hem stitch binding in place.

Wrap completed Cracker panel round card tube, insert gift/motto and paper hat. Roll up, tie ribbon!
It's a Cracker!

Short on time... Forget binding!
Make a Cracker using 'bag' method.

Follow Stages 1 - 5 pages 36 - 37.

Place Cracker panel on backing fabric **R/S together**. Pin layers. Sew round edge of panel. Leave a gap on one side. Trim excess fabric after stitching.

Turn Cracker through gap. Press well. Close gap with small hand stitches.

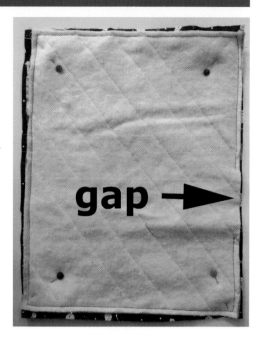

gap →

Top stitch round edge of panel:

Increase stitch length and attach walking foot to prevent layers creeping. If you don't possess a walking foot, use the regular foot. Pin edge of panel carefully before starting to stitch.

Roll completed panel round card tube and tie with ribbon.

Motto Jokes:

Q. What do you get if you eat Christmas decorations?
A: Tinselitis!

Q. Why are Christmas trees bad at sewing?
A. They always drop their needles

Q. What do you get if you cross Santa with a duck?
A. A Christmas Quacker

Stuff the turkey, peel the sprouts, lay the table, polish the silver, pour the wine, Christmas is here!

Iron Caddy

Size: 25 x 13 x 13cm (**11 x 5 x 5"**)
S/A 0.65cm (¼")

Iron too hot to put away? No room for ironing board? Make an ironing pad and heat resistant caddy. Recycle an old metallic ironing board cover or purchase a new one, two caddies can usually be cut from one new cover.

Make one Iron Caddy
One 41 x 53cm (**16 x 21"**) metallic or other heat resistant fabric
One 43 x 55cm (**17 x 22"**)wadding
One 43 x 55cm (**17 x 22"**) backing
Two 6 x 46cm (**2½ x 18"**) handles
Two 1.5 x 26cm (**⁵/₈ x 10"**) hook and loop fastener (Velcro)
4.5 x 188cm (**1¾ x 74**) binding (join strips if necessary)

1. Layer metallic material, wadding and backing fabric. Pin layers carefully.

2. Attach walking foot, set longest stitch length, sew round outside edge. (If using regular presser foot - hand tack round edges before sewing on machine - this helps to reduce the possibility of layers creeping.) Trim excess fabric to edge of metallic material.

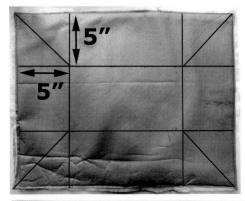

3. Working from each side, draw line 13cm (**5"**) from outside edge. Draw diagonal across each corner section.

4. Sew every line.

5. Using 6 x 46cm (**2½ x 18"**) strips make two handles (page 16).

6. Place handles on longer sides of ironing pad. Position each handle to left and right of sewn lines as shown. Pin handles in place. Stitch ends of handles to ironing pad - keep stitching inside 0.65cm (¼") S/A.

Iron Caddy

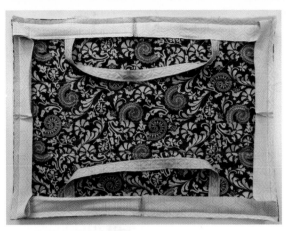

7. Working on the fabric side of iron caddy, bind raw edge. Follow page 37 - 38. Turn binding to metallic side, sew in place.

Save time and machine the folded edge of binding in place instead of hand stitching at Stage 11 page 38. Attach the walking foot. Select decorative stitch. Sew over folded edge.

8. Cut hook fastener in half. Trim one end of each section at 45°. Sew hook sections to both ends of long sides of caddy.

9. Loop fastener is sewn in middle of both long sides between hook fastener.

10. Fold up one side of caddy. Fold ends inwards, folding fabrics on stitched lines. Fasten ends to side of caddy. Repeat on other side.

11. Insert iron and then...

When you want to use pad, undo fastening and open out! Magic!

Machine Tote Mat

Size: 50 x 53cm (**20 x 21"**)
S/A 0.65cm (¼")

Tired of the sewing machine sliding about when sewing, nowhere to put notions and tools? Like to be organised? Make a Tote Mat! Finish sewing, fold it up and tidy away, hang on a peg or over the sewing machine handle - it's just sew neat! And... You can create it from four Fat Quarters!

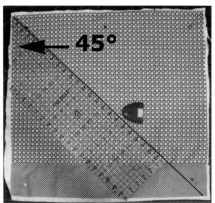

Make one Tote Mat:
One 45 x 53cm (**18 x 21"**) + One 10 x 53cm (**4 x 21"**) front
One 45 x 53cm (**18 x 21"**) + One 10 x 53cm (**4 x 21"**) back
One 9 x 53cm (**3½ x 21"**) handle
One 15 x 53cm (**6 x 21"**) + One 18 x 53cm (**7 x 21"**) pocket
Two 9 x 17cm (**3½ x 6½"**) tab
One 1.5 x 15cm (⅝ **x 6"**) hook and loop fastener (Velcro)
One 66cm (**26"**) square wadding

1. Working on front: Join the 5 x 53cm (**18 x 21"**) and 10 x 53cm (**4 x 21"**) strips together. Press seam open and flat. Place on wadding. Trim wadding to fit (keep leftover pieces). Pin layers.

2. Align 45° line on ruler with straight edge of fabric and top corner. Draw light line across fabric. Sew on drawn line. Follow page 13 and cross hatch the panel. Alternatively, draw parallel lines across fabric, sew all lines.

3. Make pocket: Sew both pocket strips together. Press seam towards wider section.

4. Fold pocket in half. Place on quilted panel. Tack (baste) using long stitch length round raw edges. Keep tacking inside S/A.

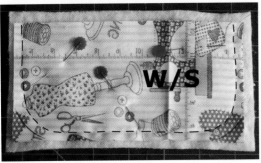

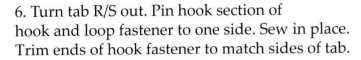

5. Make tab: Lay both 9 x 17cm (**3½ x 6½"**) tab strips **R/S** together on leftover wadding piece. Pin layers. Sew three sides (see photograph). Gently curve stitching on both corners. Trim excess fabric and wadding to stitching line.

6. Turn tab R/S out. Pin hook section of hook and loop fastener to one side. Sew in place. Trim ends of hook fastener to match sides of tab.

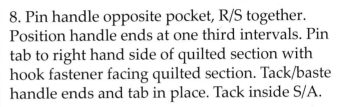

7. Make handle: Follow page 18.

8. Pin handle opposite pocket, R/S together. Position handle ends at one third intervals. Pin tab to right hand side of quilted section with hook fastener facing quilted section. Tack/baste handle ends and tab in place. Tack inside S/A.

9. Make back of Machine Tote: Join 45 x 53cm (**18 x 21"**) and 10 x 53cm (**4 x 21"**) strips together. Press seam open and flat.

10. Lay quilted section R/S down on R/S back panel. (Tote back panel 'bottom' faces pocket of quilted panel.) Pin well.

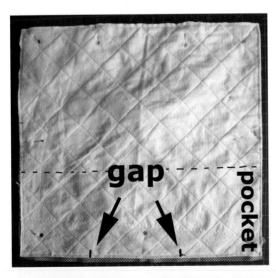

11. Sew round leaving 15cm (**6"**) gap on lower edge (pocket base). Trim all excess fabric and wadding to stitching line.

12. Turn R/S out through gap. Close gap with small hand or machine stitches. Press outside edge carefully.

13. Top stitch 0.65cm (¼") from outside edge.

14. Divide pocket in thirds. Draw light lines at these intervals. Sew on drawn lines. (For added strength, start stitching on outside edge, sew to top of pocket, reverse and sew back to outside edge. Tie/lock thread ends carefully.)

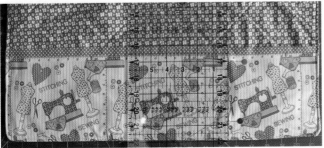

Complete Tote Mat

Put selection of tools and notions in pockets.

Fold pocket section over.

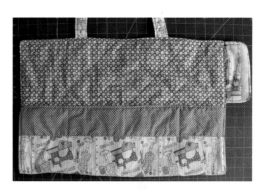

Fold left hand edge over then fold once more.

Mark position of loop fastener.

Sew fastener in place (remove tools and notions before sewing loop fastener).

Now you can sew, roll up and go!

Change the measurements and make a larger or smaller mat. Why not incorporate a pieced patchwork centre?

Patchwork Pinwheel Tote Mat: 44 x 53cm (17½ x 21")

Patchwork Pinwheel
Size: 31cm (**12½″**) square **S/A** <u>**0.5cm**</u> (**¼″**)

Cut: Four 9cm (**3½″**) + Eight 11cm (**4½″**) squares White
Eight 9cm (**3½″**) + Eight 11cm (**4½″**) squares Pink

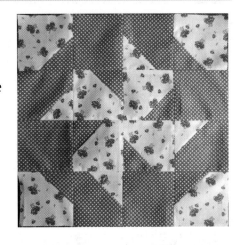

1. Draw diagonal line on W/S of one Pink 9cm (**3½″**) square. Lay this square R/S down on corner of one White 11cm (**4½″**) square. Sew diagonal line. Sew a second line of stitch **1cm** (**³/₈″**) from first line. Cut fabric between stitched lines. Open out both pieces. Press seams.

2. Repeat Stage 1 seven times.

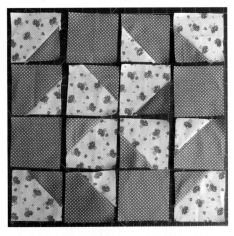

3. Repeat Stage 1 using one White 9cm (**3½″**) square and one Pink 11cm (**4½″**) square. Make three more units the same.

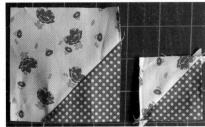

4. Using remaining four Pink 11cm (**4½″**) squares, arrange all sixteen large squares to form design.

5. Sew centre sections first then sew remaining squares into strips and attach to centre. Press completed block.

The remaining small squares can be sewn into strips and use as a border.

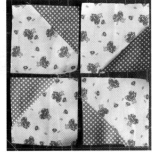

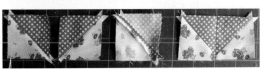

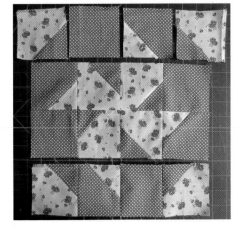

Alternatively, play with the pieces and see what you can do.

Baby Changing Mat and Bag

Size: 57 x 72cm (**22½ x 28½″**)
S/A 0.65cm (¼″)

New baby in the family? Going on holiday with an infant? Why not make a portable towelling changing mat that doubles as a handy bag? If towelling (terry cloth) not readily available purchase a new towel. **Wash all fabrics in baby friendly soap before start.**

Make one Baby Changing Mat:
One 58 x 71cm (**23 x 29″**) towelling
Twenty 16.5cm (**6½″**) squares - backing
One 9 x 53cm (**3½ x 21″**) handle
Two 9 x 17cm (**3½ x 6½″**) tab
One 18 x 71cm (**7 x 29″**) + One 21 x 71cm (**8 x 29″**) pocket
One 1.5 x 15cm (**⁵/₈ x 6″**) hook and loop fastener (Velcro)

1. Sew 18 x 71cm (**7 x 29″**) and 21 x 71cm (**8 x 29″**) pocket strips together on both long edges making a tube. Turn tube R/S out. Press tube so that the larger strip shows along one edge.

2. Lay pocket on towelling as shown. **Place pocket 1cm (½″) from towelling edge.**

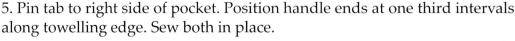

3. Pin layers well to prevent towelling creeping and stretching. Sew lower edge of pocket in place using small blanket/blind hem/zigzag stitch.

4. Make tab (Stages 5 - 6 page 43). Handle (page 18).

5. Pin tab to right side of pocket. Position handle ends at one third intervals along towelling edge. Sew both in place.

Be careful not to catch edge of pocket when sewing handle ends on to towelling edge.

6. Sew all twenty 16.5cm (6½″) squares to form a rectangle. Press seams open and flat.

7. Lay towelling section on backing R/S together leaving an even border around towelling. Pin both layers extremely well.

8. Sew round leaving gap on one edge. Take care not to catch edge of pocket in the seam.

9. Turn R/S out through gap. Press well. Close gap with small hand or machine stitches.

10. Top stitch round edge of changing mat. Take care not to sew pocket to towelling when top stitching!

11. Fold changing mat (see page 44). Mark position of loop fastener. Sew in place.

Keep pocket away from stitching - it's very easy to sew pocket to loop fastener! (I did!)

12. Divide pocket into three sections.

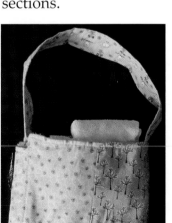

Fill the pockets with nappies/wipes and cream. Roll up into a bag and all you need is a baby!

Consider ...

Replacing the towelling with a pretty print. Quilt fabric on wadding (page 13) before making up.

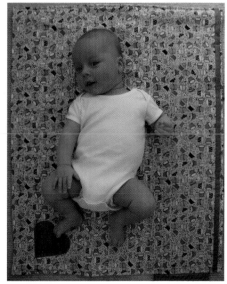

Changing Mat modelled by Harry Stone

Jennie Rayment Publications

TUCKS TEXTURES and PLEATS
Tantalise with Tucks - Beguile with Bias
Explore the fascinating world of weaving, scrunching, tucking and pleating; from the Bias Bobble to the delights of Trumpets and the Origami Twist, plus much more. Includes finishing techniques and extensive design suggestions for development. Ideal for all abilities and all ages - no experience required - just fiddly fingers! (112 A4 pages: all colour: Perfect bound.)

TUCKS and TEXTURES TWO
Fiddle with Fabric - Dip into Dye
A totally different and separate book to Tucks Textures and Pleats. Explores the versatility of Cathedral Windows, diversity of Log Cabin Corners, dynamics of Vandalism, Interlocking Shapes, secrets of Sculptured Spheres, unveils the magic of Microwave Dyeing plus projects on the Pilgrim Scrip, and other intriguing bags, Textured Landscapes, Daisy Delight, Tucked-up Circles and even the Calico Hat. (112 A4 pages: all colour: Perfect bound.)

SERGING FOR SOFTIES
Black Cats and Overlockers
A lighthearted book filled with natty notions and small projects from bags to boxes, tableware and a host of delectable delights, all suitable for the serger/overlocker although a sewing machine can be substituted. Humour rules throughout in hilarious anecdotes littering the text. Absolute 'must have' for all serger/overlocker owners. (112 A4 pages: 200+ diagrams and colour plates: Perfect bound.)

FOLDY ROLLY
PATCHWORK PZZAZZ
Tactile twiddling for all
Twelve blocks and many related projects to entrance, educate and entertain. From textured quilt blocks to bags, quags, cushions and table mats, these ingeniously simple yet fabulously folded novel techniques are ideal for all stitchers of every ability. Full colour with every stage presented in clear photographic format. Helpful hints and useful tips abound plus lighthearted tales of travel and derring-do! (112 A4 pages: 400+ photographs and diagrams: Perfect bound.)

J. R. Publications
5 Queen Street, Emsworth, Hampshire PO10 7BJ England
www.jennierayment.com